The Castles of the Rhine Valley

All Germany is rich in castles, but the romantic Rhine valley – the heartland of the old Holy Roman Empire – has a particularly high density of important medieval military buildings. Some are ruins, but many, like Marksburg Castle, have survived the ravages of war, fire and neglect in excellent condition. Today, castles like Marksburg are fascinating windows into the age of chivalry and the development of this fascinating form of military architecture.

The main function of all castles was defence, everything else was secondary. They were always surrounded by a curtain wall, which was often supplemented by a reinforced shield wall at strategic points. Crenellated battlements and arrow slits protected the defenders, and attackers often also had to overcome a series of several gates. The main entrance was protected by a drawbridge and machicolations projecting over the gate, from which boiling liquids and missiles could be dropped on the hapless foes below. The final refuge of the castle residents was the stronghold, or keep. It was the tallest and strongest building within the

Katz Castle overlooking St. Goarshausen ▽

walls, with a high entrance accessible only via a removable ladder or wooden bridge. In addition to being a watchtower and the centre point of the entire castle, the keep was also a status symbol. The main residential building (great hall) was called the *Palas*. The castle chapel was often installed in the gatehouse or one of the main towers (nearer, my God, to Thee!), and a small garden inside the walls provided herbs, flowers and vegetables in emergencies. Offices and service rooms were generally located in the outer ward.

From the 16C on castle walls had to be made increasingly thicker and stronger in response to the development of artillery. Only a few castles were made into mighty fortresses like Ehrenbreitstein, however. Instead, the nobility increasingly moved to more comfortable residential castles, usually referred to in German as *Schlösser* (singular: *Schloss*). Many, like Schloss Augustusburg in Brühl, were sumptuously ostentatious and magnificent buildings.

Popular interest in castle ruins began with the age of romanticism. In 1774, the sight of Lahneck Castle (then a ruin) inspired Goethe's famous poem "Geistesgruß". Reconstruction of many ruins began soon after this, for example of Rheinstein Castle (1825–29). Another, Stolzenfels Castle, was effectively turned into a completely new building with a strikingly unique atmosphere. Lahneck Castle, the rebuilding of which also began in 1852, was also transformed into a novel, fairy-tale structure.

Castles and stately homes are not the only attractions of the Rhine valley. Other features of this lovely landscape include romantic little towns, ancient churches with the gravestones of medieval knights and noblemen, beautiful villages and the sun-kissed hillside vineyards. Then there are comfortable hotels and inns, some actually in the castles, where you can try the excellent Rhine wine once enjoyed by knights of old. Youth hostels offer both accommodation and fun for young people and one of the most beautiful in all Germany is housed in Stahleck Castle. Castle buffs should also pay a visit to Marksburg Castle, which is the headquarters of the German Castles Association.

Tourism on the Rhine began soon after 1800. Today, millions of people every year visit this uniquely beautiful valley formed by the forces of history and nature.

KLOPP CASTLE, BINGEN

Klopp Castle, first mentioned in 1282, is Bingen's most famous landmark. The keep, probably built on Roman foundations, now houses a local history museum. Until its destruction in 1689 Klopp Castle was the home of the knights of the archbishop of Mainz. In 1713 the remains were demolished by the Mainz garrison. The keep and gatehouse were rebuilt in around 1855, the rest of the castle in 1875–79. Home of the town council since 1897. Restaurant.

MÄUSETURM, BINGEN

The "Mouse Tower" on its cliff above the Rhine was probably built by the archbishops of Mainz in the 13C as a watchtower and toll station. Enlarged in the 14C. Rebuilt in 1855 in the neo-Gothic style, served as a lighthouse until 1974. Legend has it that the Mäuseturm got its name from the fate of the hard-hearted archbishop Hatto of Mainz (968–70), who was allegedly pursued here by mice who then gnawed him to death. Actually, the name is derived from the word *Maut*, which means "toll".

◁ *Klopp Castle*

The Mäuseturm ("Mouse Tower") and the ruin of Ehrenfels Castle ▽

EHRENFELS CASTLE, RÜDESHEIM

Ehrenfels Castle, now a picturesque ruin, towers impressively over the surrounding vineyards. It was built in circa 1211 for the archbishop of Mainz by Philipp von Bolanden. Together with Bingen it formed a key stronghold of the episcopal see at the entrance to the Rhine Schiefergebirge Mountains. In 1356 it was made the court garrison of the see and was also used as a refuge in times of rebellion. The archbishops, who were also electors, often resided here, and in dangerous times they also brought the cathedral treasure to Ehrenfels for safekeeping. The castle was finally destroyed by the French in 1689. It has a square ground plan and the side facing the mountain is protected by a 5m thick shield wall (lower section 13C, upper section 14C) between the two corner towers. According to romantic author Karl Simrock the magnificent view from these twin towers is "perhaps the most sublime in the entire Rhine valley."

▽ *Ehrenfels Castle*

RHEINSTEIN CASTLE, TRECHTINGSHAUSEN

Rheinstein Castle is perched on a precipitous rock 90m above the Rhine. It was built in circa 1300 and already reached its historical zenith in 1282, when Rudolf von Habsburg sat in judgement here against the insubordinate knights of the Rhine. Towards the end of the 17C the former toll and excise station of the archbishops of Mainz lost its importance and fell into disrepair. In 1823 the ruin was purchased by Prince Friedrich Wilhelm of Prussia, who turned what was now known as Rheinstein Castle into a luxurious summer residence (1823–29). Today, the castle is owned by the former opera singer Hermann Hecher. With the help of the Friends of Rheinstein Castle Association (est. 1976) he has now lovingly restored the castle and its interior to its full former glory. There is much worth seeing, (stained-glass windows, frescoes, armour, fine furniture). The neo-Gothic chapel crypt built by Prince Friedrich Wilhelm in 1844 was reopened in 1976. The castle now has a small restaurant with a lovely terrace.

▽ *Rheinstein Castle*

Rheinstein Castle, Burgundy Garden and Rhine Tower ▷▷

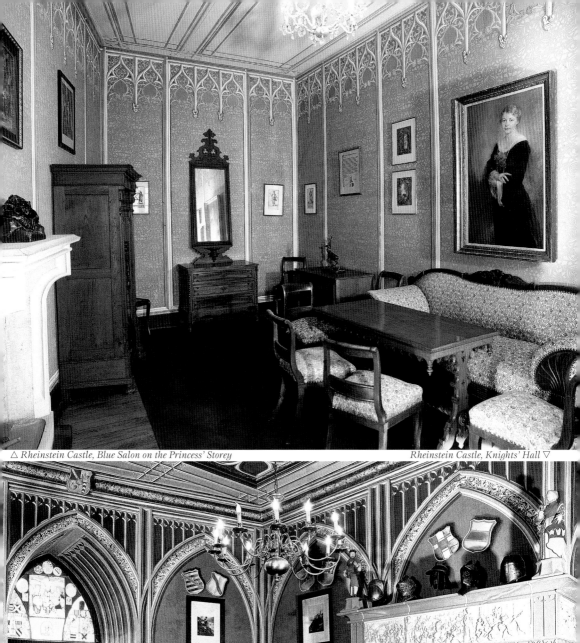

△ *Rheinstein Castle, Blue Salon on the Princess' Storey*

Rheinstein Castle, Knights' Hall ▽

REICHENSTEIN CASTLE, TRECHTINGSHAUSEN

Reichenstein Castle was probably built in the 11C to protect the estate of the Kornelimünster Abbey near Aachen. In the 13C the abbey bailiffs became notorious robber barons, resulting in the destruction of the castle in 1254 by the Rhenish League. In 1282 the castle was razed again, this time by Rudolf von Habsburg. The electors of Mainz rebuilt it in 1344, but 200 years later it fell into disrepair. In 1834 the ruin (then known as Falkenburg) was bought by General Franz Wilhelm von Barfus, who turned the gatehouse into a residence. In 1899 Baron Nikolaus Kirsch-Puricelli bought the castle and commissioned the architect Strebel to rebuild it sumptuously in the neo-Gothic style. The shield wall is nearly 8m thick in some places and dates from the original medieval structure. The interior is a memorial to the historicist style and features many valuable works of art. The private museum (weapons, hunting trophies, minerals, etc.) is well worth a visit, as is the cosy castle restaurant.

◁ *Rheinstein Castle, Dining Room*

Reichenstein Castle ▽

SOONECK CASTLE, NIEDERHEIMBACH

Sooneck Castle at the outermost tip of the Soon Forest is one of the most beautiful and without any doubt the most chivalrous of all the castles on the central Rhine. It was originally built in the 11C by the bailiffs of Kornelimünster Abbey as the outer ward of Reichenstein Castle, together with which it was also destroyed in 1253 and 1282 by the Rhenish League and Rudolf von Habsburg. The castle was rebuilt for the Mainz electors in circa 1350 and then destroyed again in 1689, probably by the French.

In 1825 the ruin was purchased by the Crown Prince and later King Friedrich Wilhelm IV of Prussia, who had it rebuilt as a hunting lodge from 1834. In the Middle Ages castles were usually plastered and painted in bright colours, but the romantic rebuilders preferred to see the undressed stone; the ruins were regarded as complete in themselves. The core of the square main castle probably dates from the 12C. Attractions in the interesting interior include fine Empire and Biedermeier furniture, Rhine landscapes and weapons. Don't forget to visit the castle pub!

▽ *Sooneck Castle*

HEIMBURG CASTLE, NIEDERHEIMBACH

This castle overlooking Niederheimbach is a very imposing sight. In the 13C Count Palatine Ludwig the Severe wanted to expand his domain southwards from Bacharach. To gain access to the territory of the Palatinate by Kreuznach he acquired and rebuilt the castles of Sooneck and Reichenstein. The archbishop of Mainz countered this by building Heimburg Castle. Completed in 1305, it was originally known as Haneck ("Wood Corner") or Hohen-eck. Heimburg lost its strategic importance in 1344 when Reichenstein Castle was ceded to the archbishop. It became the residence of officials and then fell into disrepair in the 16C. At the end of the 19C the ruin was acquired by the Stinnes family, who renovated part of it. The castle has a semicircular ground plan with the apex of the crescent facing the attack side. The modern residential structure is built against the original thick shield wall. Heimburg Castle is now in private ownership and used by the owners as their home.

Heimburg Castle ▽

NOLLIG CASTLE, LORCH

Nollig Castle ("The Watchtower") on its high cliff over the Rhine valley is actually the north-west bastion of the Lorch town walls. Originally built in circa 1300 as a fortified half-timbered tower, the structure was then clad with heavy slate masonry in the 14C, and the filling in the spaces was knocked out. The outlines of the original wooden framework are still clearly visible inside, particularly on the north side (now behind a new interior wall), together with a block staircase. In 1936 the castle was bought by Fritz Wild, a gemstone cutter from Idar-Oberstein, who began his stylish renovation in 1939. On the mountain-facing side the massive residential tower has a reinforcement resembling a shield wall (no arrow slits or smaller windows) with large towers at the corners. The castle has no curtain wall of its own as this function was performed by the town wall. It is now privately owned. Beautiful view of the entry of the Wisper into the Rhine.

▽ *Ruins of Nollig Castle*

FÜRSTENBERG CASTLE, RHEINDIEBACH

The ruins of Fürstenberg Castle stretch up picturesquely into the sky from the surrounding vineyards. It was built in 1219 by the archbishop of Cologne to protect his property around Bacharach. The county passed to the electors of Wittelsbach in 1215, and they then sought the enfeoffment of the castle, which was granted by the archbishop in 1243. In 1410 Fürstenberg Castle became a full part of the Kurpfalz domain. The castle was besieged and taken by the Spanish in 1620 and again by the Swedish in 1632. It was destroyed by the French during the Palatine war of succession (1688–90) and has been in a state of decay ever since. The castle is protected by a massive shield wall. The high, circular keep from the 13C tapers towards the top. The walls on the Rhine side are the remains of a residential building. We can also see parts of the curtain wall and extensive remains of the medieval plaster, which provides an inkling of the original colourfulness of such buildings. Fürstenberg is now also privately owned.

Ruins of Fürstenberg Castle ▽

STAHLECK CASTLE, BACHARACH

This beautifully situated castle overlooking Bacharach was originally part of the domain of the Episcopal Electorate of Cologne, but the bailiffs who held it in fief later drove back the power of the archiepiscopal see. The castle's first known feudal lord was Goswin von Stahleck, mentioned in 1134. His son Count Hermann married a sister of King Konrad III, who made Hermann count palatine in 1142. His successor Konrad von Hohenstaufen created the Rhine Palatinate after being granted additional property by his half-brother Emperor Barbarossa. In 1194 Konrad's daughter and heir Agnes secretly married Heinrich the Welf (son of Heinrich the Lion), who inherited the Palatinate in 1195. The castle was destroyed by the French in 1689. Between 1925–67 Stahleck was converted into what is probably Germany's most beautiful youth hostel. The shield wall, keep and residential hall are an impressive example of the Hohenstaufen castle-builder's art. The moat is filled with water, which is rare for mountain castles. The castle bailey is now open to the public.

▽ *Stahleck Castle*

PFALZGRAFENSTEIN CASTLE BY KAUB

Resembling a massive stone ship ploughing through the waters of the Rhine, this defiant castle has an interesting history. It was originally a toll tower like the Mäuseturm in Bingen (q.v.). In 1327 Pope John XXII excommunicated King Ludwig the Bavarian for demanding new and exorbitant tolls from travellers at Kaub Castle (Gutenfels). Ludwig's second crime was the construction of this new and extremely mighty tower, which was designed to enable him to enforce his accursed tolls all the more effectively. The protective wall around the tower was built in 1338–42, the bastion at the southern end and the interior arcades in 1607. In 1793 the German army under Colonel Szekuly crossed the Rhine here, and the famous General Blücher did the same with his troops on New Year's eve of 1813/14. Perched picturesquely on its rocky promontory in the Rhine, Pfalzgrafenstein has a ground plan in the shape of a bridge pier. It was never taken – the strong current of the river here made the castle impregnable. Interesting old furniture and fittings.

Pfalzgrafenstein Castle and Gutenfels Castle ▷▷

GUTENFELS CASTLE, KAUB

Gutenfels Castle dominates the hillside overlooking Kaub. It was built in circa 1200 by the ministerial officials of Falkenstein-Münzenberg, at imperial behest. In 1257 the Falkensteins controlled Kaub, the castle and the Rhine tolls. They then sold their rights to the Pfalzgrafen (count palatine) bei Rhein in 1277. King Ludwig the Bavarian was very fond of the castle and he held court here several times in 1326. In 1504, during the Bavarian-Palatine war of succession, the castle was besieged unsuccessfully for 39 days by Landgrave Wilhelm von Hessen, which earned it the name Gutenfels ("Good Rock") from the early 16C onwards. Soon after this the woodwork and masonry were auctioned off (1807, 1813). Archivist Friedrich Habel then bought the ruin in 1833 and saved it from destruction. In 1888 it was acquired by the architect Gustav Walter, who renovated it in 1889–92. The core structure, an important example of Hohenstaufen military and residential architecture on the Rhine, dates from around 1200. The castle now houses a hotel.

▽ *Gutenfels Castle*

SCHÖNBURG CASTLE, OBERWESEL

It is documented that the massive complex of Schönburg Castle was owned by Hermann von Stahleck in 1149. Later it passed to the archbishop of Magdeburg, whose bailiffs and castle lords were the imperial ministerial officials of Schönburg. By 1266 no fewer than five families of the lords of Schönburg were living in the castle, and it became a *Ganerbenburg* – a castle owned jointly by several families. In 1342 the property was divided in three and each third was then subdivided again. Schönburg Castle was destroyed by the French in 1689. In 1885 the ruin was purchased by the New York banker J. J. Oakley Rhinelander, whose forebears originated from the Rhineland. He renovated parts of the building in the period until 1920. In 1950 the castle was bought by the Oberwesel city council, which initiated further construction work. The castle is perched on a narrow rocky ridge with a truly massive shield wall, one of the most important of this kind. Today, Schönburg Castle houses a hotel with a restaurant and a private gallery. A youth hostel has been built next door.

Schönburg Castle ▷▷

KATZ CASTLE, ST. GOARSHAUSEN

The full name of Katz Castle ("Cat Castle") overlooking St. Goarshausen is actually "Neukatzenelnbogen". It was built on a projection of the Loreley massif by the counts of Katzenelnbogen, at some time before 1371. It passed to the landgrave of Hessen in 1479 and played an important role in the defence of the landgrave's property on the Rhine against the neighbouring Electorate of Trier. In 1626 the Elector of Cologne besieged the castle, which was courageously defended by Captain D. Suale, who only capitulated when expressly ordered to do so by the landgrave of Hessen. The castle was blown up by the French in 1806. In 1896–98 it was partially restored under the direction of senior privy counsellor and district administrator Berg. The residential building stands on the tip of the rocky spur on the Rhine side. It is flanked by two corner towers and the curtain wall. The keep is still a ruin. After serving as a holiday home for a national social institution for a few years Katz Castle is now owned by a Japanese businessman.

▽ *Katz Castle*   *Katz Castle and the Loreley Rock* ▷▷

RHEINFELS CASTLE, ST. GOAR

The expansive complex of Rheinfels Castle overlooking St. Goar was built in 1245 by Dieter von Katzenelnbogen. In 1255/56 the Rhenish League besieged the castle unsuccessfully for one year and 14 weeks in response to an increase in the Rhine tolls. The castle became the residence of the counts of Katzenelnbogen and was the site of lively cultural activities. In 1479 it passed to the landgraves of Hessen. Wilhelm III von Hessen-Kassel had it made into a fortress from 1497–1527, and Philipp II von Hessen-Rheinfels (1567–83) installed a magnificent royal residence. In 1692/93 Rheinfels was unsuccessfully besieged by the French, which put an end to their attack on the Central Rhine. In 1794 the castle was then surrendered without a fight to the French, and in 1796–97 it was blown up and then used as a quarry. The oldest section is the central castle, whose ground plan is still visible. The ditch was roofed over between 1497 and 1527, creating the biggest vaulted cellars in Germany. The underground passageways were added in the early 17C. Around one third of the complex has survived and now houses a museum, a restaurant and a hotel.

MAUS CASTLE, WELLMICH

Maus ("Mouse") Castle overlooking Wellmich was one of the most advanced castle complexes of its day. The name was a humorous jibe at neighbouring Katz ("Cat") Castle and the powerful counts of Katzenelnbogen. Construction was begun in around 1356 by Archbishop Boemund of Trier, who also lived here occasionally. His successor Kuno von Falkenstein (1362–88) completed the castle. Both Kuno and his successor Werner von Falkenstein (1388–1418) died here. Maus Castle was originally called St. Peterseck and later became known as Deuernburg (Thurnberg). In 1806 it was auctioned off for demolition. In around 1900 it was bought by an architect called Gärtner from Cologne, who renovated it between 1900 and 1906. The castle is protected by a massive shield wall into which the keep is integrated. The great hall is on the south side, a residential tower on the west side. Today the castle is still privately owned and it houses a historical falcon and eagle station. During the summer months there are daily falconry demonstrations with interesting lectures.

Rheinfels Castle overlooking St. Goar ▽

THE WARRING BROTHERS, KAMP-BORNHOFEN

The picturesque castles of Liebenstein and Sterrenberg probably became known as the "Warring Brothers" because of the way their front battlements face each other, as though they were standing off for a fight. Sterrenberg Castle was probably an imperial castle before 1110 and in 1195 the emperor granted it as a fief to the lords of Bolanden, who collected imperial tolls here. In 1492 Sterrenberg was still the seat of an authority of the Electorate of Trier, but by 1568 it was already in a state of decay. Between 1968 and 1978 it was secured and partially rebuilt by the German Monuments Authority. Liebenstein Castle stands above Sterrenberg. In 1294/95 Count Heinrich von Sponheim-Dannenfels sold one half of the castle to each of the two lords of Sterrenberg, who forthwith referred to themselves as "von Liebenstein". The castle is perched on a narrow ridge, which gives it two main lines of attack. The remains of the keep (13C) stand on a projecting rock. Restaurant in the 14C residential tower.

◁ *Maus Castle*

The Warring Brothers ▽

MARKSBURG CASTLE, BRAUBACH

One of Germany's most beautiful castles and the only intact hilltop castle on the Central Rhine. Probably built in around 1100; in 1231 it was held as a palatine fief by the lords of Eppstein. In 1283 it passed to the counts of Katzenelnbogen, who resided here occasionally. The castle was inherited by the landgraves of Hessen in 1479. In 1803 it fell to Nassau, in 1866 to Prussia. In 1900 Emperor Wilhelm II bequeathed Marksburg Castle to the Association for the Preservation of German Castles, which still owns it today. Marksburg provides fascinating insights into the age of chivalry with all the standard features of a medieval stronghold, including its own garden, wine cellars, kitchens, ladies' bowers, knights' hall, chapel, armoury and a grisly collection of instruments of punishment and torture. Marksburg is the home of the German Castles Association, which works to preserve Germany's castles, and it is a popular meeting-place for castle fans. "Knights' banquets" are served in the restaurant and you can buy original medieval documents at the castle shop.

▽ *Marksburg Castle · Kitchens*

Marksburg Castle ▷

Marksburg Castle　△ Knights' Hall　▽ Battery Courtyard

STOLZENFELS CASTLE, KAPELLEN

Stolzenfels Castle is one of the most outstanding extant examples of neo-Gothic architecture. The original castle, first mentioned in 1248, was built by Archbishop Arnold II. of Trier (1242–59) as an instrument for imposing his illegal tolls. It was then destroyed by the French in 1688/89. In 1802 the ruin passed to the Koblenz city council, which gave it as a present to Crown Prince Friedrich Wilhelm of Prussia in 1823. He had the castle rebuilt using plans drawn up by Karl Friedrich Schinkel, with the help of Johann Claudius von Lassaulx. Friedrich August Stüler also worked on the project (1836–49) after Schinkel's death. The king moved into the castle in 1842, dressed ceremonially in old German costume. In 1845 Queen Victoria of England stayed at Stolzenfels, which was used as a royal guesthouse. Most of the remains of the original castle were preserved in the reconstruction project. The sections on the Rhine side were linked to a single unit and the residential building at the rear was enlarged and connected to the Rhine wing. Interesting works of art.

▽ *Stolzenfels Castle* *Stolzenfels Castle / Pergola in the inner courtyard* ▷▷

MARTINSBURG PALACE, OBERLAHNSTEIN

Martinsburg castle stands on the bank of the Rhine in Oberlahnstein, which received its city charter from King Ludwig the Bavarian in 1324. The castle was also built around this time as a Rhine toll station for the archbishop of Mainz, together with the town fortifications. From 1719–21 Archbishop Lothar F. von Schönborn converted the castle into a Baroque residential Palace. Today it is owned by Dr. Johannes Romberg, who maintains and preserves it. The former water castle at the south-west corner of the town walls is a picturesque ensemble of buildings arranged around a square bailey. The pointed arch gate with portcullis in the east wall features a fine cast oriel with French designs and a coat of arms (1395). This is also the entry to the beautiful bailey. The main rooms were apparently in the north wing. The ground floor features a cross-vaulted roof and at the north-east corner a chapel with a small choir oriel. One tower now houses the Lahnstein Carnival Museum. Parts of the Oberlahnstein town fortifications have also survived.

◁ *Stolzenfels Palace / Queen Victoria's room*

Martinsburg Palace ▽

LAHNECK CASTLE, OBERLAHNSTEIN

Lahneck Castle stands on the slope just above the entry of the Lahn into the Rhine. It is a classic example of Rhine romanticism, combining medieval fortifications, additions in the English neo-Gothic style and precious fittings and furnishings. It was built before 1244 by the archbishop of Mainz and destroyed in the Thirty Years' War. In 1774 the ruin inspired Goethe's famous poem "Geistesgruß". It was rebuilt under the direction of the chairman of the East Rhine Railway Society, Morarty, starting in 1852. Today, most of Lahneck Castle is once again a residential complex. Its symmetrical ground plan attests to its origins in the late Hohenstaufen period. The chapel's stained-glass windows date from circa 1400. Queen Victoria's portrait (by Franz Xaver Winterhalter, circa 1840) still hangs in her room. Other items of interest inside the castle include a portrait of Friedrich the Great by Antoine Pesne, fine furniture, porcelain, ceramics, a 15C kitchen sink and a fully furnished three-storey doll's house (19C). Restaurant.

Lahneck Castle ▽

RESIDENZSCHLOSS, KOBLENZ

The first and still most important early classicist building in the Rhineland was built in 1777–93 by French architects for Elector Clemens Wenzeslaus of Trier. In the course of time it served as a military hospital, a barracks and a court of law. It was the favourite residence of Prince Wilhelm of Prussia (particularly from 1850–58) and his wife Augusta. The palace was destroyed in 1944 and rebuilt in 1950–51.

▽ *The Residenzschloss*

DIKASTERIAL BUILDING, EHRENBREITSTEIN

The Dikasterial Building is one of the surviving adjoining buildings of Philippsburg Palace, which used to stand below Ehrenbreitstein Fortress. Formerly the seat of the electoral court of law, it was designed by Balthasar Neumann and built by Johannes Seiz in 1739–48. The elongated structure with rhythmically arranged walls and roofs is extremely artistic. Two lions holding the electoral coat of arms stand between gables of the central projection, above them a statue of Justice.

EHRENBREITSTEIN FORTRESS, KOBLENZ

In the period after 1815 Ehrenbreitstein was one of the mightiest fortresses in all Europe. The original castle was built in around 1000 by Heribert, a scion of the Salian-Konradian dynasty. Soon after 1018 it was acquired by the archbishop of Trier and used occasionally as his residence. Over the years Ehrenbreitstein became an impregnable fortress integrating all the latest developments in military architecture. Although it was never taken it was destroyed by the French in 1801 and then refortified by the Prussians after 1815. Friedrich Wilhelm III's plans were based largely on those of the original fortress, but much was also new – for example the ramparts were replaced by rows of casemates. Perched on a precipitous rocky cliff, Ehrenbreitstein towers 118m over the Rhine, opposite the mouth of the Moselle. The fortifications have plain rectangular forms. Today the fortress houses the Koblenz State Museum (exhibitions on the development of technology on the Central Rhine), the State Archives and a youth hostel on the lower eastern side.

▽ *The Dikasterial Building*

Ehrenbreitstein Fortress ▷▷

CASTLE OF THE ARCHBISHOPS, ANDERNACH CASTLE

The castle of the archbishops, now a picturesque ruin, is a typical town castle. In addition to controlling the Rhine valley it also served to maintain power over the town itself. This was also the reason for the loopholes facing the town on the west side of the powder tower. In 1349 it was demolished in a rebellion of the local citizens against the archbishop of Cologne. Their quest for freedom failed however, and in 1367 Archbishop Engelbert had the castle rebuilt at the citizens' own expense. Later, probably in 1496, he also had it reinforced. In 1689 Andernach Castle was destroyed by the French. The former water castle at the south-east corner of the town is integrated in the town fortifications. The older parts (circa 1370) are made mainly of basalt lava blocks, the more recent (circa 1500) of rough stone masonry. Most of the massive main tower dates from the earlier period. The great hall dates from 1370; its west wall abuts the heavy circular powder tower (circa 1500), which in turn is connected to the town walls.

▽ *Castle of the archbishops – Andernach Castle*

△▽ *Ruin of Drachenfels Castle and restaurant*

DRACHENFELS CASTLE, KÖNIGSWINTER

Visible for miles around and steeped in legend, "Dragon Rock" Castle is one of the most picturesque and romantic of all Germany's ruins. In a declaration dated 1147 Archbishop Arnold of Cologne stated that he had built the tower and part of the other buildings and transferred the castle to the Cassius Foundation in Bonn to protect its property in the region. Construction was then completed by the foundation's provost Gerhard von Are (1126–69). The lords of Drachenfels, whose coat of arms featured a fire-breathing dragon, appeared on the scene in 1176. They held lesser dominion over Drachenfels, most of which was on the west side of the Rhine. From the 13C on, the trachyte quarries here were very important for building work on the lower Rhine and Cologne Cathedral. Drachenfels is one of the most significant early castles in the Rhine valley. The ruin and its restaurant can be reached on foot, by donkey or with the lovely rack railway. The Romanesque keep made of rough-hewn trachyte blocks was built in around 1140. Its south-west corner is collapsed.

DRACHENBURG PALACE, KÖNIGSWINTER

Drachenburg Palace, located below Drachenfels Castle, is an important example of historicist architecture. The site was acquired in 1879 by Stephan Sarter and the palace was built from 1882–84. The plans were drawn up by the Düsseldorf architects Bernhard Tüshaus and Leo von Abbema and then revised by master builder Wilhelm Hoffmann in Paris. The interior design is by Franz Langenberg from Cologne. Sarter, the son of a brewer, was born in Bonn in 1833. In 1857, after a stint at a bank in Cologne, he moved to Paris, which he came to regard as his home. In 1881 he was made a baron. In 1945, after a chequered history, the palace was in quite a sorry state. It was saved from ruin by art dealer Paul Spinat, who had the buildings and park rebuilt in 1971/72. The style of Drachenburg Palace is modelled on medieval castles. One of the more outstanding features of the magnificent interior is the colourful stairwell with many large historical paintings. The "Burghof" restaurant stands just opposite.

Rhine panorama with Drachenburg Palace, Ruin of Drachenfels Castle and Rhöndorf ▽

GODESBURG CASTLE, BAD GODESBERG

The isolated basalt peak high above the town on which the castle stands was once the site of a Roman fortification. The medieval castle was founded in 1210 by Archbishop Dietrich of Cologne. It was then enlarged in 1244 by Archbishop Konrad of Hochstaden, who also started the construction of Cologne Cathedral. Archbishop Walram enlarged the complex again in around 1340. In the 14C it was often used as a summer residence for high church officials. It was blown up in 1538 during the war of Truchsess. In 1959–61 a hotel and restaurant designed by Gottfried Böhm were integrated in the ruin. Remains surviving from the original 1210 structure include the exterior walls of the great hall and the keep. The lower level of the keep was probably built in around 1244 (the supporting stones of the original wall-walk are still visible); three additional storeys were then added in circa 1340. The Chapel of St Michael is integrated in the outer ward. The apse dates from the early 13C, the choir tower and nave were built by Archbishop Josef Clemens in 1897–99.

◁ *Drachenburg Palace*

Godesburg Castle ▽

POPPELSDORF PALACE, BONN

Poppelsdorf Palace (Clemensruhe), based on a ground plan by Andrea Palladio, expresses the epitome of a garden schloss. The original medieval building on the site was a water castle with four wings, which was acquired by Archbishop Walram of Cologne (1332–49) and used frequently as a residence for the archbishops. It was demolished in 1657 after serious war damage. Construction of the present building was started in 1715/16 by Elector Joseph Clemens. Guillaume Hauberat supervised the work; the plans were drafted by Robert de Cotte. The elector's death interrupted the project, which was finally completed in 1744–56 by his successor Clemens August, under the supervision of Balthasar Neumann. It has been part of the university since 1818. Poppelsdorf Palace is a four-winged complex with projecting corner structures and a beautiful arcade around the circular inner courtyard. The palace itself now houses the mineralogy and petrology museum of Bonn University. The botanical gardens were installed in 1819, and the garden palace is the home of the Botanical Institute.

▽ *Poppelsdorf Palace*

AUGUSTUSBURG PALACE, BRÜHL

Augustusburg Palace, one of the most important stately buildings in Germany, features some masterpieces of interior decoration, including the magnificent staircase and the fine stucco work. In 1284 Archbishop Siegfried of Cologne built a water castle here as a bulwark against the city of Cologne (completed 1298). It was blown up by the French in 1689, and in 1725 Elector Clemens August commissioned Johann Conrad Schlaun to build him a new palace. From 1728 onwards François Cuvilliés continued the work on the building in the Regency and early Rococo style and also modelled the west side. The staircase, one of the most beautiful in Germany, was created by Balthasar Neumann in 1740–46. Augustusburg Palace is a three-winged structure built around a magnificent parade ground. The eastern front side of the north and south wing, designed by Schlaun, is one of the most important works of the German Baroque. The west side with the gallery tracts was designed by Cuvilliés, as was the south facade facing the gardens. Part of the park has now been restored to its former Baroque glory.

Augustusburg Palace ▽

SEVERINSTORBURG CASTLE, COLOGNE

The city fortifications of medieval Cologne were the most massive and extensive in the entire Holy Roman Empire, featuring the most advanced military architecture of the day. In the early period Cologne used the original Roman fortifications. In 1180 Archbishop Philipp von Heinsberg then started construction of a ring wall enclosing all outlying villages and several abbey complexes, with fortified gatehouses protecting the entrance roads. The semicircular course of the original walls is still visible along the remains of the old ramparts. Parts of the walls, particularly the gatehouses, still survive. One of these is the mighty Severinstorburg, started after 1200. It has a rectangular base with a barrel-vaulted archway and a massive tower topped with battlements. On the field side are two small side towers with gun emplacements (late 16C) and one of the four surviving wall sections. The other surviving gatehouses are also worth seeing: the Ulrepforte, the Hahnentorburg (one of the biggest of all medieval gatehouses built after 1200) and the Eigelsteintorburg.

▽ *Severinstorburg Castle*